THE PROMISE CLINIC

ROBERT SAXTON
The Promise Clinic

ENITHARMON PRESS LONDON
1994

First published in 1994
by the Enitharmon Press
36 St George's Avenue
London N7 0HD

Distributed in Europe
by Password (Books) Ltd.
23 New Mount Street
Manchester, M4 4DE

Distributed in the USA
by Dufour Editions Inc.
PO Box 449, Chester Springs
Pennsylvania 19425

ISBN 1 870612 39 6

The text of *The Promise Clinic* is set
in 10pt Walbaum by Bryan Williamson, Frome,
and printed by
The Cromwell Press, Broughton Gifford, Wiltshire

ACKNOWLEDGEMENTS

Some of the poems in this collection have previously appeared in:
*Faber Poetry Introduction 7, London Magazine, New Spokes,
New Writing Two* (Minerva/British Council), *Oxford Poetry,
The Observer, Paris Review, PN Review, Poetry Review, The Spectator*
and the *Times Literary Supplement*.

'The Promise Clinic' won joint first prize in the TLS/Cheltenham
Festival of Literature Poetry Competition, 1988.

'The Manatee and the Dugong' borrows factual details and a few
phrases from an article in *World* magazine (February 1988) by
Heather Parker and Jasper Clough.

The Enitharmon Press gratefully acknowledges a grant from the
London Arts Board towards the production costs of this volume.
It also wishes to express thanks to the University of Sussex for
financial assistance through the Ralph Lewis Award.

For my parents,
Joyce and Colin Saxton

Contents

Caveat Emptor

Some books, however thin,
Refuse to fit back in their slot.
That's when a friend will zero in
Across the bookshop floor
And put you on the spot.
Oh yes, what's this? A present? Who's it for?

Your secret self, that's who;
And so you feel just as you might
If the shower were to run dry, leaving shampoo
On your hair, helmet of foam,
And you with just a squash racket to fight
A dragon on the bus ride home.

ONE

Foraging

You probably haven't noticed
That every steeple has a tiny ladder
Right up to the weathervane.

On the older churches –
Say, pre-1400 – these ladders
Will take only a child's weight.

So there I was, climbing
To the base of the stork's nest
With my hipbag full of feathers.

Miles away, the river was
A silver thread carelessly dropped
Across the quilted fields.

The white dots were villagers
With flags happily furled:
Madame Stork was still

In the next parish, foraging.
The hardest part was letting go
Of the ladder with both hands

To clip the harness round.
For a few seconds
I hooped the ancient octagon,

Leaning into the stonework
As I fiddled with the clasp,
My cheek cold against a rung,

And my head, as I pushed away
And turned it, suddenly scratched
By twigs, which startled me –

It felt like my grandmother's
Fingernails ambushing me
In the one place I hadn't thought of.

The Rainy Season

That autumn, the year we moved to the attic flat,
I gathered leaves – every brown and yellow shield
Around the line-post. You bought me a bobble hat
In Arsenal's colours (we'd relegated Sheffield

To oblivion). I mounted the best leaves
On balsa frames. The grimmest days of heaviest rain
Were those I liked. Gloves dancing from my sleeves,
I'd slip down quietly. The gurgling drain

No white man had ever seen, the breathy park,
The cockatoos upset. Later through the trees
You'd come, mock-angry, calling in the gibbering dark,
Breasting the monsoon, homing towards my warrior shriek.

Your small truth rippled in its own breeze.
You brought it in and held it to your cheek.

Mohicans

All summer long I trailed Mohicans
On the hammer ponds,
Crouching, watchfully heroic, in the shade,
Parting the willow fronds
To follow the slow progress their canoes made
Across the silken water, laden with guns

They had traded from the policeman for a squaw
Who would sew his silver buttons on,
Teach him to track thieves
By bending his ear to a stone,
And strew his bed with scented leaves;
Or carrying the raucous girl next door

Snatched from her garden swing,
Expertly gagged and tied,
Her waist-length hair stroked and stroked
By braves no less wide-eyed
Than she, while those in the second boat joked
Loudly in their curious tongue, paddling

Close for a better look
At their prize, the paleface stranger.
Hatching rescue plans, I'd jog ahead,
Ducking branches, alive to the danger
Every time I snapped a twig or landed
With too loud a thud on the far bank of a brook.

The woods were striped with gold, a gold cage,
Light meshed with dark like mistletoe
In the oaks' high boisterous scrum
Of leaves. If the sun's joy is shadow,
This was the sun's true home,
A book of natural law turned to its first page.

It was around here my father would walk
Grumpily with the dog on days
When the atmosphere at home had turned
Intolerably sour. It might be his pipe's blue haze
Smoke-signalling above the ferns
That I'd see first. Sometimes I'd stalk

Them for half an hour or more till
The panther caught my scent and came
Crashing unstoppably through the brush –
Geronimo! – a black engine with a tongue of flame
Leaping (Mother would say 'making a fuss')
Straight for my throat, to drink its fill.

Mother said men and women were at war.
I knew the truth of this from stiff goodnights,
The skirmishes and silences, the glisten of tears
After talking about having gas, or fishing rights.
Nothing at home had been quite right for years.
I dreamed of the policeman with his squaw,

All smiles beneath their blanket
Stitched with love-knots, caribou, crescent moons.
Autumn's arrows rattled in their quiver.
The nights grew cold, the afternoons
Held pits of apprehension, making me shiver,
Crouched in my willow thicket,

And feel my whole life lurch to the dark
Of winter, school, the hell of maths and play,
Long evenings in. Running behind time,
I took a shortcut through the deepest woods one day,
And the light dying from a giant oak left me a lingering sign
That hurried me on: a cock and balls carved in the bark.

High Becquerel Farm

This is my den,
The oiling pen
Where sheep are oiled
Against the wind –

Or so I said
To little Ted,
The townie
Staying on our farm.

It was quiet, to say
It was a bank holiday.
Ted knew why: this year
Everyone had gone to Chernobyl.

We sat here in the cold,
The ruined fold
Hugged round us
Like a blanket.

Damned if I'd show
Him my patch of snow
The winter had left behind,
Dirtier than ever,

Or my favourite tarn
The Innominate Tarn
All churned up
Like the view from a galleon.

River Red With Berries

In Wildman's Wood a river flows,
A river red with berries.

Where is she gone, where is she gone?
And why is she away so long?

She's picnicking in Wildman's Wood
On leaves of hornbeam, oak and beech,
Which all taste best when they are brown.
(Remember she was old and thin
And couldn't keep her supper down?)
She's picnicking the branches clean.

When will she come back again?
I miss her, so I need to know.

When will she come back again?
When the river runs milky with melted snow.

The Alligator Hotel

The square was a fat purple leech
Intent on the evening, bruising the light

Around the yellowing tent where minute by minute,
More and more the star, my aunt performed her act

Of grace and charity, click-clacked her love,
My mother's love, to keep me from the cold,

Oblivious to the dark which seeped like poison gas
Up between the floorboards of the house,

Her room that was once her sister's room,
My mother's (as close to being there

As not being there can be), and mine
Dishevelled with an orphan's grief.

Another knitting pattern from the beyond
Was coming through: alligator jaws propped wide,

Red lobby set in a green façade,
Twin epauletted doormen standing by,

And round the sides and back, and round each arm,
Loops of taxis, each with its little boy inside.

TWO

Esperanto Spoken

A Girl Sleeping

What might not she know?
One day she might turn to me
    when I've dropped a plate
    and lash me with a stream of backslang.
One day she might read
    in a newspaper
    of someone's capture or release
    and rush out of the flat
    without a coat.
But probably, in a month or so,
    we'll be conversing fluently
    in a dialect of Esperanto.

Bad Language

*Before he left he locked
    a hive of language in my head,
    most of it bad.
I lie in bed with my window open –
    like a courtroom at the weekend,
    cleaned, exhausted, raw,
    submitting to the judgement of the stars,
    douching in a milt of asterisks.*

White Water

Excitement is passing through our lives.
In the big wind we roll like tumbleweed.
   Signposts are white ghosts,
   Maps are stroboscopic flaps,
Whereas, before, they merely disagreed.
We roll and catch in the forecast gale.
A froth is passing through our lives
Like the white patch travelling up your fingernail.

Wrong Holiday

Manoeuvres I utterly failed to understand
At first now dimly sketched a meaning:
Something on offer, something planned
For us both if I dare – a private screening
Of truth, or in some psychic game a hand
Leaning the way her hand, luck, life were leaning,

Instead of the way my life was leaning
Then – back on itself, she gave me to understand –
So that when she consented to my trawling hand
The obvious seemed too crude a meaning
For what was perhaps an alibi, a bonus screening
The real purpose of what she'd planned.

Like someone on the wrong holiday, I planned
Strategies of forbearance, leaning
On the wind with a lying smile, screening
Myself from suspicion. No one would understand.
The film would keep the secret of its meaning.
Close to my chest I hugged my foolproof hand.

A Motel Room Near St Austell

.... when you do dance, I wish you
A wave o' th' sea, that you might ever do
Nothing but that, move still, still so,
And own no other function.
                    The Winter's Tale

Venetian blinds are battened,
Though it's only just turned noon.
The bedside globe is smooth and white –
A prelapsarian moon.

The duvet's docile on the floor,
The hollow in the sheet's still warm.
A tigress, or a giant hare,
Has just this minute left its form.

Unseen, the mountains hoard their myths –
Benign, spectral, recondite.
Their useless gifts are bobbing near,
Borne in on tides of light.

Her shape, like parian when still,
Is flowing now across the room
Towards her weightless underwear.
She flickers in the milky gloom,

And to such flickering one is drawn,
Like hand to fur, or cup to lip.
Where I had meant to smooth, I scare,
And drown where she had thought to sip.

A Malachite Egg

Now I know what the egg means: it's a living
thing before it has time to get messy.

Two ponies stand
Perfectly still,
Head to tail,
Tail to head,
Each tail
In its turn
Swishing flies away.

We are in a lane
Two fields
From the cliff edge,
Smiling goodbye,
Face to face,
Our bicycles
Enforcing distance.

I remember this,
Sitting alone
In my kitchen,
Weighing in my palm
The cold object,
Weighing in my mind
Its wavy stripes

In two shades
Of green,
Its singleness,
Its perfect hold
On time,
And this evening
When I walk

Along the beach,
Crunch by crunch
I shall
Turn over,
Like the waves
The pebbles,
This first promise.

Blind Love

Dark gathers
In this wood
Without weather

Hours before the sun
Slips into its
Blindside run.

Blackbirds drink
The light in secret.
Dippers risk their blink

Beside the stream,
Bibs darkening
Until their gleam

Fades from sight
To memory softly
Printed by the light

That lingers yet
Behind the eyes; which
In a while I shut,

And when I look again:
No change, or hope
Of change.

Black static
Floods the eyes
With panic;

As when we drift awake
At first light
And some opaque

Form, a pillow
Or a lover, blocks
The window

We expect to find,
And makes us think
We're blind.

The Makeshifter Calls

He was an hour late
   and that was an hour of worry.
Nothing was going right
   and no one was even saying sorry.

Everything was makeshift, unreliable,
   as I'd explained to my GP,
   whose Freudian face and lovely surgery
   (Victorian globe, leather books, serpentine couch)
   had made me think, naively, he might be of some use to me.

So I'd looked in the *Yellow Pages*
   and chosen the largest, most pictorial ad,
   a firm with three telephone numbers and the prefix Euro-.
We never close, all credit cards taken, it said.

He turned up at the same time
   as my notorious on-the-run lover.
His leather case was scarred like a favourite toy
   and smeared with butter from his previous call
   where he'd amiably plonked it on the tea table,
   over the muffins, before pulling out
   all his little springs you attach yourself to the future by.

Devil's Prothalamion

Brace the will to take the strain.
Weigh the in-laws with the bride.
Lies enlarge inside the brain.

Damn the Abel with the Cain,
Fell the Jekyll with the Hyde.
Brace the will to take the strain.

Scotch the hymeneal stain
That claws its way from side to side.
Lies enlarge inside the brain.

Check the harvest grain by grain,
Cheat the bloating of the tide.
Brace the will to take the strain.

Both sides of the counterpane
The clans are grouping where you lied.
Lies enlarge inside the brain.

Plan to catch the stopping train.
Let self-protection be your guide.
Lies enlarge inside the brain.
Brace the will to take the strain.

Mirror Friends

The first thing is you learn to fall.
Then when you meet your mirror friend
You'll find it doesn't hurt at all.

Let schnorrers check the wherewithal,
It's always fun to overspend.
The first thing is you learn to fall.

You'll need some kit for volleyball
(If you're ball-stupid just pretend,
You'll find it doesn't hurt at all)

And clothes to climb the waterfall.
And if you slip, that's not the end:
The first thing is you learn to fall.

Maybe your voice is somewhat small,
And needs a little more Southend.
You'll find it doesn't hurt at all.

Yes, change is brilliant, overall.
Why stick to one side of the bend?
The first thing is you learn to fall.
You'll find it doesn't hurt at all.

Thousand-Island Dressing

A twist in my belt gave us away:
   It hadn't been there ten minutes earlier
When we went upstairs. There followed
   A chase through the azaleas and
The slender silver birches. Oddly
   Enjoyable this, dodging the father
And she, in her long flimsy dress,
   The holly's lecherous lower branches.
It was just what I needed as it made
   Her hobbling father and the whole business
     laughable.

Then he got caught up in the lawnmower
   Lead, which gave us time to get the Morris
Started – it was pointing downhill.
   We got to the caravan in the small hours.
Then next day on the phone to the bank
   To fix up the transfer and *her* bank
For emergency funds, a shopping spree
   In Colchester for clothes and luggage,
A Chinese dinner by lanternlight, then
   Up with the lark to catch the flight from
     Heathrow.

Now we're well set up. We've a thousand
   Islands at our feet, and there's a club
Where eloped couples meet, and swap
   Their stories. She's been writing to her
Father, and I've reason to suspect she's been
   Using his name for me, her 'Pocket Romeo',
But that's all right. She's great in bed,
   And wears the clothes I like. Sometimes,
With another couple, we go for walks along
   The waterfront, looking for Hong Kong's
     two junks.

Crossroads

I'm standing at the window feeling the cold air on my face.
Flocks of cloud tear across the full moon. The wind flutes
In the hearth, the treetops rustle like presents being unwrapped.
Below, one of the dogs shuffles her chain on the concrete.
Our lamp's off, so through the window I can plainly
Make out the woods and fields humped in the dark,
Restless and full of villainy. No doubt the poachers' wives
Are all alone, asleep or listening already for the latch.

Farr will be netting trout. The Potts twins will be out
Ferretting. They have a ferret strong enough to fight
A back-kicking, stubborn buck, but sometimes he kills
And lies up in the hole. You try burning gorse to smoke him out,
And if this fails you have to use another ferret with a line
And, following the line, dig along the tunnel to the kill –
A long night's labour. Maybe tonight they've put the muzzles on:
If you're disturbed and have to show your heels,

A muzzled ferret left in the wild will starve to death,
But there's no such risk on the gamekeeper's wedding night.
I can guess where *they*'d sooner poach tonight. ''Tain't trout
'E'll be ticklin', that's for sure': I know the way they think.
In fact, exhausted by the dancing, still in her clothes,
Charlotte lies fast asleep, love in reserve, sprawled
On the four-poster her mother improvised from beanpoles
    and lace.
A lace swag threaded on a pole sways above the window.

Brent Geese at Pagham Harbour

Pure movement, aerial muscle above the fosse.
Honks float down over the isogloss.
It's land and sea, of course, not sky, they cross.

Going, gone, leaving a secret sense of loss,
A wren-sized albatross. Feathering hands, we toss
Observations sidelong across the isogloss.

A Farmhouse Interior

I never walk the fields empty-handed.
From whatever field I happen to be leaving
To whatever field I happen to be entering
There's always something to carry,
If only a scarecrow's hat or neckscarf
Whose turn it is to be rotated.

Back home there are sheets to be rotated.
(When I awake it's seldom empty-handed.)
In my wardrobe I keep a silk neckscarf,
One I stole when she said she was leaving.
On walks to the fields I still carry
A tie to knot in the woods before entering.

I came back late this evening, and entering
The cottage felt sick. The kitchen rotated.
I've had a little more ale than I can carry.
I was paid today but came back empty-handed.
There were jeers in the pub as I was leaving,
And some reference to a lady's neckscarf.

So I'm drunk and I stagger to the neckscarf.
What new life could she think she was entering
That made it so quick and easy leaving?
Change rooms and the hurt's rotated.
Will she find this and end up empty-handed?
She can curse but her curse will never carry,

Any farther than my curse would carry
When the neighbour's lad came with her neckscarf
Expecting not to leave empty-handed,
With an open-handed grin on entering
That on listening to me suddenly rotated,
Shrivelling to embarrassment on leaving.

It's time that I gave some thought to leaving.
There's no shortage of logs to chop and carry.
The weathervane has violently rotated
And a gale tugs hard at the scarecrow's neckscarf.
From the hearth comes a deathly chill on entering.
Yet I'm leaving the woodshed empty-handed.

The Night of Invincible Hail

Messages mangled.
Bill-drifts in the hall.
Ecosystem tangled.
Brylcreem on the wall.

Coxcomb unspangled.
Hangdog, male.
Singleness wangled.
Thereby hangs a tale:

Love-throat strangled
The night of invincible hail.
Angelfish angled.
Leechless go the pale.

Away From It All

Stillness and closeness, merely, make a place –
A circle mulled in the wilderness.
Heather springs back, rock bears no trace.
This is by day. By night such places,
Silted with darkness,
                              trail their provenance
Unhopefully on the mind's turbulence
But now and then, like flares, weakly fluoresce.

Collapsed in the huge wing chair's embrace,
I strain to gather in the dark, the emptiness.
The pub's fire folds into its ashes.
This is my circle, mulled in the press
Of self-erasing images.
                              Realigning loss,
I strain for a small piece of her sadness,
The wilderness in which I made a place.

Lawn Aerator Sandals

Today in the Gardeners' Hyperdome
I sauntered along the avenues admiring,
Right and left, ingenious flimsy things for gardening.
I'm sure you would have seen the charm
Of the pair of lawn aerator sandals with screw-in tines,
The kind of present you might have bought – two pairs – for
    our new home,
Whose lawn we could have aerated walking up and down, arm
    in arm,
Enjoying the cherry blossom. They were designed to strap
Over ordinary shoes, my size 11s and your incredible size 4s,
Which on train journeys you would beg me to pull up on my lap,
Undo, and remove to massage your feet.

And bouncing on their bamboo poles,
Responsive to the breeze from automatic doors,
Morning's Minions, the rubberized kestrel bird scarers
We could have posted round the cherry trees in flocks
To scare real birds away. And should our turf
Have proved a habitat for inconsiderate moles,
Why not a battery-powered device whose drun-drun-drun of
    shocks
Below ground would have sent them scuttling to the next
    postcode
With a ringing in their ears? Too cruel, I hear you say.
You would happily have watched our too well-aerated lawn
Like a building site accumulate soil by the cartload.
It's obvious to me that moles, like birds, are vandals.
But if you had thought that moles were underfoot,
I doubt if we ever would have worn
Our lawn aerator sandals.

The Promise Clinic

First day

They flutter on the eye,
A mild surprise,
Like prices on books
Lent long ago
You thought you'd never see again.

But more than these
The thickening of ghosts
You'd starved of light.
Who would have guessed
They'd interview so well?

Second day

First, all the whisky's under lock and key.
You can smell tomorrow's weather,
Hear your babbling bloodstream, see
A corkscrew hair trapped in the cleaner's charm bracelet.
She swabs and jingles her way across your floor,
Out of your room and down the corridor.
You're alone. Now try this for size:
Your first, worst marriage, whole before your eyes.

OTHERS

Dissolution

The vast ruined nave is famous for its blackberries.
Here the abbot was put to the sword: a stone
Hidden among brambles marks the spot. A ghost's batteries
Run down just like our own batteries. This one
Has turned up much too often to be visible,
Yet someone blackberrying alone might feel skin prickle

And head back for the car, believing it's just
That the children will be wondering about tea.
And so, ungathered, lovely ripe berries gather dust
All night – that outdoor dust we never see
Dulling a surface as we see indoors, more widely travelled
Than dust in a room, and not so easily controlled.

The Angel Roof

Blythburgh 1644

Above our heads, moored in their plash
Of stars, apart,
Unregarded, watching us strain
At the massive vehicle of our faith
Stuck in the years of change,
The angels rode.

We argued. We were confused. Hearts liquid
With fear. An old man
Caught with beads by his bed
Was sentenced to beating hemp for a month.
Many whispered the old language
Under the new.

Each ship that hove into view
Seemed larger
Than the last. Our shrunken harbour yearned
For salt. Some families found help
In worm-eaten books hidden
Beneath their floors.

One day a small ship touched our shores,
Landing horses and men.
We had to pay to have our own brass removed.
Gunsmoke possessed the slanting
Broken light. They proffered
Mock courtesies,

Uttering deliberate gibberish.
Suddenly the angels
Looked pained, pitiful, and the moment before
The bullets rattled home
Turned, some said, to wood; others,
To flesh and bone.

A Drink in a Country Churchyard

The green-room stillness of yew
   And the mossy reclining stones
We love to have about us drew
   Me from the bench outside The Crown
To finish my beer on a raft of bones.

All summer's warmth pressed
   On my face. I floated half-awake,
Then, rolling, saw a woman dressed
   In mourning drink me in, a frown
Like a trout-rise in a black lake.

Lying there I felt not shame,
   Only a vague dread of some surprise
Impending. Then other people came,
   As if they'd heard my wish:
A pleasant couple with pork pies,

Their little girl drumming her knife
   And fork idly against her plate,
A Belgian cyclist and his wife,
   Two London lads debating where to fish,
All ventured through the lychgate,

Stopped, looked round, then made
   Their way along an avenue of graves,
A parting in the shoal of dead, to shade
   Or sun, and worked out how to sit.
Talk, laughter, came to me in waves.

A table tomb hosted a domino dance,
   Each little black headstone
Commemorating some lost chance,
   Perhaps a failure of nerve, or wit,
Or welcome, or testosterone.

The ale was a local brew, Black Friar.
   I took into my mouth a garden
Of tangled flavours, like the shire
   Itself folded in my throat, a vale
Of hops, barley, oak, acorns – Arden.

I yawned, stretched. Bones are an old map
   Hung inside us, though we steer
By different means. They turn to scrap.
   It wasn't here the dead might trail
Their scarves into our atmosphere.

Stoning Byron's Ghost

Avenging ivy padding up the wall of the Abbey's west wing
Could only be part of a masterplan to rescue posterity
From a curling, yellowing, nonetheless dangerous manuscript
Locked in the tower. Otherwise, while the estate was emptying
Of tenants (sick to death of living on the master's charity),
Falling into disrepair, filling with weeds and being stripped

Of all its remnants of prestige, year by year this book might
    gather
Strength, occasioning at first postscripts in letters, or
    conversations
Amid rumours of cigar smoke after dinner, then with ease
    finding
Subscribers, whose sons and grandsons might see the thing
    spread farther
Than could have been imagined, in multiplying editions and
    translations
And ratified by every kind of leather, cloth and paper binding.

But more likely these are just my uncle's ramblings, tall tales
For which, struggling with speech, he couldn't find listeners
    any more,
Legends of childhood, a handful of vivid lifelines, like the time
He was replacing slates on the east wing roof after a night of
    gales
And the zealous gardener tidied away the ladder lest it be an
    eyesore
To the master's lunch guests assembled in the morning room –

Discussing, perhaps, the hair's-breadth survival of the orangery
When their talk was stopped by a clearing of the chimney's
    throat,
A tumble of bricks and a shower of soot pronouncing a gruff
    'ahem'.
Before you could say 'knife', laughter was rippling through the
    company
Circled round the boy on the hearthrug in his ragged,
    blackened coat,
Shyly gulping wine (his first and only) from a glass with an
    air-twist stem.

And wasn't it the same year, another night of blustering March
Winds, though less tumultuous, that five or six villagers
     walking home
Around midnight through the tunnel of trees down the
     woodside lane
Past the Chapel vowed they'd seen, framed by the side-porch's
     Gothic arch,
A ghost in frenzy – brilliant sobering white in the moonlight's
     monochrome.
Breathlessly, in the parlour, they told their tale. It was a thing
     profane,

Surely it was Byron's ghost agonized by a fit of longing or
     remorse,
The cruel, demonic man. Had it not been for his gammy leg,
     you'd have sworn
They'd not have got away with Christian souls still roosting in
     their bones.
Next morning the sexton found, trapped between the vestry's
     double doors,
Hanging limp like a shot-filled seagull, a surplice, dirty and
     torn;
And at its foot (or so my uncle claims) blood on the scattered
     stones.

The Stunted Oakwood

Toiling up the slope of moor
   Towards the stunted wood
Suddenly we came into the breath
   Of it – a gnarled, rustling,
Beckoning thing, which judging by its size
   Should still have been
A field's length away, as if
   We had caught ourselves
Betraying secrets hours too soon,
   Getting aroused before we knew
Each other's histories.

Such tangled places make me think
   Of nations like Old Japan,
Baroque in welcome yet
   The furniture so interrogatory.
You could be naked there,
   And much admired, but only
By keeping perfectly still.
   Clambering in sleeping
Dragon's heat, green shadow,
   Two giants, bruising ourselves,
We'd lost all instinct for such nuances.

Upstairs

The view from the Regent's Gallery, at dusk:
Two miners knocking off, slouching
Up the gravel path by the lake,
Unwary commandos,
Starting the Chinese geese honking,
And the head gardener's dogs barking,
And the envy-alarm in our young butler's heart.

The Life of the Slug

This creature's habitat
Is the rank gardens
Of university towns
Where the warped pages
Of forgotten, rotten diaries
Like ancient jungle cities
Afford to the scarcely living
A home that commemorates
Superior civilization.
And sometimes voices

In the garden recapture
The same events, supernovae,
Reversals on the river,
Trial by celluloid, even
The bride stripped bare
By her bachelors – voices rich
With foreknowledge of sex.
Which makes our sexless creature
Stir inside his sleeping-place,
Dream of being a professor

With a brief to invite
The brightest students to tea,
And wide awake that night,
After moon-rise, squeeze
Beneath the french windows
And limp across the carpet
Towards the foot of the stairs,
Fadingly, a wounded archer,
The life-blood pouring
From his heel in a silver trail.

Looking Forward, Looking Back

Window shopping, the tilting of prams at the kerb,
   the imperceptible flirtation of traffic wardens,
   continued as always, everywhere.
A redcoat in a doorway received a quiet dressing down.
The war fitted quietly into the life of the town.

We started on the shady side, boisterous, untrained,
   frankly a mob, always falling out over the obvious,
   tearing a photo, anything, out of someone's hands
   for a better look, or faces collapsing with envy
   when one of us showed off a tag of valiant colour
   newly stitched onto the drab uniform.
Not surprisingly we failed when we tried to take
   the sunny side by storm.

The matinée crowd, blinking in the glare, poured out
   between the golden columns of the theatre.
We could saunter across and back whenever we liked,
   but this of course was a hollow victory,
   like tearing a telephone dialling code booklet in half:
   no one noticed, or if they noticed cared one iota.

The birthdays came in ones and twos,
   like magpies or, for sorrow or joy, jailbreaks.
Everyone knew: a nimbus of embarrassment circled
   the heart full of pride, and the enfranchised one
   would smile amid the lank, shy handshakes.

Week by week we were diminished, each coming of age
   the tautening around us of a belt of time,
   till we became, no longer home, the majority,
   but a pathetic bunch of castaways.
We squinted at the sunny side,
   watching our old companions haggle in the market,
   while piously we counted off the days.

Their clothes were grey, barren of rank,
  their faces gravely civil, white as sheets.
Their ribbons lay quiet in drawers
  like the courage light in the hearts of our milkmen
  still delivering milk on our mean streets.

Esperanto Nights

Agreed: this is no place to bring up children.
At twelve or so the sons are trained for fighting.
Camouflage and hatred smudge the difference.
Mothers relive their bravest hour embracing
Their eldest (*now* their eldest) in the restaurant
Where, over the prettiest, officers pick quarrels.

I've heard some foul language in these quarrels,
Words that must surely brutalize the children.
There was once an ugly scene in the restaurant
One night when I was working. Two men fighting,
Cousins it turned out, seemed to be embracing,
Till one pulled away with a knife. What difference –

Cousin, lover, enemy, husband – what difference
Can there be? Our enemies, though now our quarrels
Are at white heat, our hatred all-embracing,
Used to meet us on the road and grin like children,
Show photos of their eldest and, fighting
Their shyness, pledge to meet us at the restaurant.

What evenings we had in that restaurant!
Plain-cooked meat, but the herbs made all the difference.
Lovely herb-smells trampled out by the fighting
Infiltrate our room and start new quarrels
With history. We curl into ourselves like children,
Trusting the power of yearning, of embracing.

That's how the daughters manage – by embracing,
In jeeps, or filthy rooms behind the restaurant
Where officers in knee-length shorts like children
(In the dim light it's hard to tell the difference)
Shed humanity like clothing in their quarrels,
Tossing money in the mud to get them fighting.

Beyond, in the green ring of the fighting
Around the township, two claws embracing
Show the blessings that pour on mended quarrels.
Outside our room: the neon of the restaurant.
Let's try to sleep, forget about our difference,
My womb-dream of the sweet bruise of children.

Those cats fighting sound like starving children.
Crooning and quarrels drift up from the restaurant.
We lie frightened, embracing – there's a difference.

The Age of Chivalry

This crossing was our chance to manufacture
Peace in our lives, the quiet cure of the sea.
We forget how dreams mark easily – bowels
On fire, a child's sabotage, and now the world's.

Of the twinkling fiancée we are envious,
Pleased to explain the rules of engagement,
To a novice in our mystery bring a message
From the higher sphere of cots and kitchens.

We try to guess the shape our future takes.
Inside ourselves, all this talk of war
Awakens a muddled, muffled, contrary spirit
Waiting a lifetime for a change of weather.

The children are our 'young moderns'. We gather
Them up from games on deck for the captain's
Admiration. Secretly, we've schooled them so
They'll grow into a world grown out of war,

And women at last will have some… elbow room.
Meanwhile, despite ourselves, we're reassured:
Husbands air their gravest doubts even to wives,
Dressing for dinner, colliding in our cabins.

Three backward-sloping funnels manufacture
Clouds, trailing behind us over the dark sea.
A Linotype machine juddering in the bowels
Rumbles out the ship's news, and the world's.

Dining on sea cow, smiling, a touch envious,
We read of the captain's surprise engagement.
Our compliments to the chef: the message
Travels on its devious route to the kitchens,

Unimaginable as the route our food takes,
Inside ourselves. All this talk of war
Has made us sociable, happy to spirit
Some romance out of boring tropical weather.

Everyday our two busybody reporters gather
Gossip for the front page. The captain's
Behaviour has become princely, hammingly so.
There will be war, yes, but only a short war.

We tend to stay up later in the smoking room,
Editorializing, swirling brandies – reassured
The world will be kept intact for our wives
And children stowed away safely in our cabins.

The Café-Bookshop

It's taught in schools: how the equestrian statues
Were lethal, the riders were all wanted men,
And one opened a slot in the belly of his horse
And hibernated there, waking to the river distantly
Cracking and fussing like the preparations
Grandparents make. He welcomed himself
As a hero, limping into the spring sunshine.
Under the new dispensation statues were pedestrian.
In the brass of the night he stood like a drunk
Signposting uselessly under the map of stars.

Pedestrian statues lie broken, remembered,
The most public ridden by the children of children.
This one who is pasting snot into bronze nostrils,
He is hungry and cold, like a skater who has left
His lunch behind; yet his eyes are bright
With the infamous glissades of revolution.
Our city looks new-made, as under a fall of snow.
Teachers are chatting to parents in the streets:
Note the frisson of joint enterprise when the sons'
Names are pronounced. Daughters are also mentioned,

Their days off work, their love letters uncrumpling
On the fire. We all mutter the hurtful song,
The *samizdat* hymn in the blood. We have lived long.
'Hey, face-ache!' Rough words laden with love,
Spoken by a father who has roused himself
From a daydream, a great tumbledown thaw of books,
Fielding, Trollope, Galsworthy and the rest
Of those who knew the burden of masculinity,
All the solitary souls patient in a café-bookshop,
Which breaks into a smile when the rain starts.

Remembrance Day

My hands are fumbling
Among the garden's last things.
I can just reach the ground.
   Every blasted joint hurts.
For gardening and such
   I wear old rugby shirts.

Our TV is London's
Last working valve museum.
Even the whispers buzz.
   A wreath schlepped by a toff:
He shambles in, trailing
   Red mud. He turns it off.

I'm outside again,
Wounds in flower, remembering
To be merely a kennel
   For the old porcupine,
For the storm in his head
   Deep in the storm in mine.

The Life of the Salmon

An old man climbing the ghyll,
    Thirsty, scarred by shops,
His rainbow gleam in shreds,
    Flops into peace: a gilt emporium
Stuffed with riding crops, shooting sticks,
    Hallmarked shaving sets.

At school he was the salmon boy
    From the second Michaelmas term
When he arrived with no luggage, bearded.
    Unbefriendable, he vaulted
Out of our gang to some rare honours
    Without loss of wildness.

Any parents would handle with awe,
    As if they'd a god in their charge,
Any child missing so many months.
    He shivered off love
Like a stallion stumbling out of the river,
    Right where you were fishing.

Your salmon now is oceans away,
    There's no one to finger the gash,
The awkward contours of the lips,
    When in a voice like the old King's voice
He orders an umbrella made up
    In the school colours.

The Shingled Roof

The minutes overlap
To make a shingled roof,
A slope of aspirins
Over all our headaches.

I've turned my back on it
A thousand times to you,
Or we've lain quiet and still
Planning our arguments.

We've touched a thousand ways,
Like summer leaves touching,
Managing to fight clear
Of wounds and surgery.

As the shingles rot, one
By one I replace them.
Now we boast every age
Of wood from green to black.

We extract memories from
Each other like splinters.
Yet sometimes when I reach
For my pen or the phone

Suddenly I'm back there
In the deepest dark woods,
All purpose gone:
Dr Alzheimer, I presume.

The Lighthouse

The lantern
To prove the Earth is round, three teachers and all of our class
    borrowed from my uncle a six-oared gig, *The Guiding Star*,
    and beat our way through the waves
    until the lantern was all that showed of the lighthouse.
We drank oxtail soup from thermos flasks.
No one was quite persuaded.
Next day a group of us founded the Flat Earth Society,
    dedicated to all forms of constructive mischief.
My mother said, A club needs a logo.
I doodled for an hour after tea.
The one she chose was a lighthouse,
    streaming solid light from its head,
    earthed on a cairn on a flat horizon,
    our gig, like a beetle, sprawling underneath.

The handrail
The point of the lighthouse is the spiral brass handrail
    as much as the whipping lantern.
One day my uncle the lighthouse keeper felt a pain in his chest.
An ambulance lumbered along the country lanes,
    brushed by hedges, siren wailing.
For three weeks his rag hung on its hook at the top of the stair,
    which would normally mean he was at home:
    he used to polish the handrail every time he came or went.
Day by day it dimmed, breathed on by neglect.
When he returned there was no rag at the bottom of the stair,
    and besides he was weak
    and had to be helped by the ambulance driver.
It was a rare journey, spiralling back like this
    along the trace of his own farewell.

The rocks

When possession of wild birds' eggs became illegal,
    antiquity was deemed no excuse.
If you'd inherited a collection,
    the authorities advised it be destroyed.
Detectives raided lofts, airing cupboards,
    anywhere redolent of incubation.
My uncle's will revealed he'd hidden his twelve metal boxes
    under the rocks piled at the lighthouse base.
In some the labels were in his own rough hand,
    in others a watery copperplate, perhaps that of my
        grandfather,
    who spoke of twite's eggs in a letter to my uncle of the 1930s,
    signing himself, Your ever-loving father.
Reading these words I thought of my mother,
    and for a moment wondered how it was she had been
        usurped.

Victoriana

Bivouacked on a jagged rock a pelican piously
Disbursed a mash of sprats to eager young,
Pressing its bulging bill-bag to its breast.

Our son tortured Latin labels on his tongue,
Riding shoulders to the level of the domes,
Proud like the turbanned leader of a caravan.

At six he was taken by the whooping cough.
The name put me in mind of a soaring swan,
Our Sinbad a silhouetted frog, diminishing.

A soul can shrink and lose the body's touch.
Sharing a bed, we haunted a ruined sacrament.
A pair of ghosts, we walked through solid grief.

In time we could speak calmly of our quest.
In one parlour a whatnot exhibited souvenirs,
Quite ordinary things, nutcrackers, pens,

As if a meteorite were just a lump of coal.
Meanwhile he'd learned, almost, to spell.
Poor girl, she moaned, her arm a phonograph's.

'Rescue this poor creture of God.' We did,
And never again called upon her gift,
Not needing to: he dwelt in her, angelified.

Brought to the birds she let warm tears fall,
For the sparrows, the drab avian underclass,
And for the finches forced into such finery.

Fish Christmas

On the first day we had brill
With vermouth. She'd had trouble with the car,
She was tired, it was true, yet her sullen face,
Her downcast eyes, I felt, betrayed some deeper ill.

On the second day we had char
Baked in the Loir style. When she said grace
Her voice quavered as if she'd dared to kneel
Secretly that morning at some forbidden altar.

On the third day we had dace
In ale batter. Love itself is the salve to heal
The heart's wounds, proffered as God's firm handshake.
After coffee she scuttled off in her carapace.

On the fourth day we had eel
Pie with mussels. I lay awake
Much of the night, talking to God, praying
To know what suffering her rudeness might conceal.

On the fifth day we had hake
Chowder. When I tried steering
The talk to her unregenerate husband, Mike,
She ran up to her room, pleading a headache.

On the sixth day we had ling
With sweet and sour sauce. Some spike
Lodged in her heart was turning Siobhan
Against me. In starvation's shadow still robins sing.

On the seventh day we had pike,
Her favourite. She was up at dawn,
Weeping quietly in the kitchen. I went to investigate
But got short shrift. I sorted recipes, businesslike.

On the eighth day we had prawn
And Jerusalem artichoke salad. She ate
And said little but after coffee rallied,
Blooming unexpectedly – a winter-flowering thorn.

On the ninth day we had skate
In black butter. Her talk was much more fluid,
More relaxed. I trod warily, ever on the lookout
For ways to end this unbearable stalemate.

On the tenth day we had squid
Cold in aioli. A calm, neutral day, no doubt
The best that I could hope for. By now I'd grown
To accept she thought me dull, meddling, stupid.

On the eleventh day we had trout
Au bleu. A silly quarrel blew up. She'd flown
Into a rage, really for no reason. So shrill,
So cruel, her words. This was trouble I could do without.

On the twelfth day I dined alone,
On meat again – a succulent mixed grill.

Bereft of every needle, gift and star,
The tree rises from its green sea like a fishbone.

Radio Ga-Ga

We're confident you won't see through us yet.
We're selling lamps for just your brand of dark.
At least we're seeming to, in silhouette.

But crouched inside the outline of the ark
We've been at work, eating the alphabet.
First the two defenceless a's in aardvark...

Till by midnight we've pulled it off, no sweat,
We're munching zeds, in fours, with a wry spark
And crackle, snoring quietly. We're all set,

Our madness woven like a watermark,
Or plain lies in a book of etiquette:
The first transistors dreaming of the park.

Reflections

A Tabloid for the Wee Small Hours

Live Letters

Tell me (my schooling's full of holes)
What firemen use to grease their poles.

I' truth, sir, no grease keeps 'em slick:
The firemen's trousers do the trick.

Teacher praised who plimsolled rumps.
Quick, lads! All hands to the pumps!

Let's give the metalwork a shine!
The flames lick round the plimsoll line.

Star Wrinkles

Keep vigil with insomniac rust.
Open the telly: meet the dust.

Break bread with the brave bright mouse
Whose wee black pellets dot the house.

Shall the sigh wear out its sheath,
The teacher or the fire chief?

The moon looks blankly on their throes,
Turns on love its cold white hose.

Hard heart, soft bargain: play it rough.
The valves accumulate their fluff.

Baby, You're So Friable

Boffins agreed on cranial sumps.
It seems brain cells sheer off in lumps,

Not slow depletion byte by byte –
Great colonies lost overnight

Like tons of chalky cliff that slide
Quietly into the nibbling tide.

Warning from the Bookmark Council

It has come to our attention
That you have trespassed in the south,
Which probably explains
The forbidden fruit stains
In a yellow scream around your mouth –
Just a minor point we wanted to mention.

We have also been advised
Of your character-building trek north,
Where breath freezes
And tropical diseases
Learn hardiness. You found the broth
Small consolation and the fruit impossibly priced.

We have located a surveillance
Report filed on your foray west.
Their day is only later, not longer,
Nor is the life-force stronger
On the boardwalk. Your quest
Came to nothing – peaches and cream and rollerskate
      maintenance.

A stringer with a hypersensitive nose
Has been sniffing out your lotus-capers in the east,
In a tinkling pagoda you learned about
From some guru back west, no doubt,
Cross-legged all day, your mind fermenting like yeast,
Burrowing to the heart of a sacred book you never close.

Aren't you a bit too old for this palaver?
You are close to the eternal velleities,
The chronology of lost grace,
The time it always took to find your place,
But shouldn't you be thinking about your eyes?
We can send you a bookmark, if you'd rather.

Anglaiseries

Beyond the stepping stones and the stone lantern
  and the gather of bamboo and the little stream
  awaiting paper boats of camcorder instructions
  in knockabout sanserif English
  lies the lawn where English visitors in cream trousers
  mistake pastiche for obeisance.
When they dive for the ball it's the real kamikaze dive.
Here are some picking sides, playing in the stainmaker's craw
  like Tokyo metropolites eating round the poison of a fish.

Animals in Architecture

Remember Gran's canary in its cage? – a tragic case.
  Nell and her plastic playmate seemed to fill it.
I pitied the wee wretch its lack of aerospace.
    Taking tea there on Fridays in a rain of millet
    (The kitchen was tiny too) I thought up ways to kill it
Out of kindness. Warfarin? Gas? However Nell reacted,
Death in the wild would, of course, be more protracted.

It's a natural law: the drab despise the vivid.
  Rook Ku Klux Klans hunt exotic escapees,
And gays make boring hetero males quite livid.
    Bee-eaters brought up on millet can't catch bees
    Any better than giant pandas speak Chinese –
So in any case captivity's a widening catastrophe,
Turning sweetness of freedom sour as instincts atrophy.

People in touch with animals – petowner, policeman, farmer –
  Have no excuse for consciences not heightened.
Our view now is holistic: cruelty's rotten karma.
    The starved can slip through bars, we're frightened
    Still, but try to empathize. Enlightened,
We forge bonds *with*, not *for*, break off enslavements,
Make *space* for them – like holes for trees in pavements.

The Farmyard Crocodile

Settled in one of the crypts or vestries
    Carpentered like a bureau's secret drawers
In the ziggurat of hay in the great dutch barn
    Shortly I'll lay my head. If you come by
With your torch and see my shoes in the corridor,
    Look in on me: see that I've come to no harm.
From my attic of hay I've been watching you
    In the failing light, alone down there
In the farmyard, too distressed at having lost
    The fluorescent green crocodile they bought you
At the fair to notice the change coming over
    The animals. While you've been staring down
Into the black water of the cattle trough,
    Into which you could no sooner plunge your arm
Than you could plunge it into solid rock,
    Their storybook slave-clothes have been melting,
And their eyes, large and small, have started
    Their bore-holes into our comfortable night.
After you've gone to bed, shall I clamber down
    The giant steps of the ziggurat and creep
To the cattle trough, very quietly so as not
    To spring open their eyes? In the morning
You'd be amazed to find your toy on the stone rim.
    In the cave of your hand (I'm dreaming now)
It might even glow again, but altered forever,
    Like an animal's eyes after its first beating,
In which our offences smoulder like the wasted years.

Treasure Island

The camp has places to watch videos, play bingo,
    Buy women, lose them to high-rollers.
      When I strayed into this habitat
    In the wrong plumage, an old hand with a macaw
On his shoulder put me straight: 'Hey caballero,
You know why we chop trees? Our people gotta eat,

'Is why. Trees keep us poor.' So nature's a quango
    Endlessly shuffling forms. Where dollars
      Like wasted fruit fall and rot, what's
    To be done but turn conquistador
And pluck them for the cash ecology? As in a panto,
The parrot squawked its echo: 'Pieces of eight!

'Pieces of eight!' The parrots pluck at tidbits of lingo
    Tossed aside by hombres of many colours
      Like the trees chewed and spat
    By vegan slaves of carnivores, going on before.
To a parrot all speech is Esperanto,
As to a locust all things green are meat.

The Manatee and the Dugong

The manatee: sounds like an obsolete
Aristocrat versed in flamboyant formalities.
The Spanish Church declared her fish, not meat,
Commandeering a delicacy for Fridays –
Such delicacy as grossness magnifies,
Bolted-on crust of barnacles and algae,
Grey-green submersible streaming seaweed and flies
Columbus took for mermaid hair in 1493

Off Haiti. Too much grog. Yet there's a poetry
Easy to evoke, an almost pastoral mood,
The sea cow grazing its water meadow, placidly
Chewing the cud of its favourite food,
Water hyacinths – a hundred kilos a day.
Teeth trundle from the rear in a second wave
Relieving the line worn down, in disarray.
(Typically, manatees can be expected to have

About twenty sets of teeth before they die.)
In the fetid deltas of the Everglades
Just below the surface you often see them lie,
Their backs all rutted from propellor blades,
Crisscrossing scars half-voluntary like sunburn.
Young animals born in a manatee reservation
And released into the wild fail to learn
Skills of feeding, wintering and navigation

They'd have picked up cruising for several years
At their mother's side. Hence their poor success.
They flounder – out-of-control bathyspheres
Lost in the wrong latitudes, flapping distress,
Risking hypothermia where the sea drops to 20 degrees
Centigrade, because of their slow metabolic rate.
Where other creatures loll and play, they freeze,
Despite thick skins and moderate layers of fat.

Amazonian hunters apply zoological mechanics.
When the manatee surfaces for air, two long
Bamboo pegs are plugged into her nostrils. She panics.
(She's unable to breathe through her mouth.) The dugong,
Her only relative, suffers similar violence
Off New Guinea, held underwater in a rope sling
Until she drowns. The dugong: sounds like a dunce,
A bumpkin clapped in the stocks merely for existing.

Wild Food

One wears a bandana,
White spots on a red ground,
Narrows his eyes to the road's horizon
Like a Soviet poster icon
Thirty feet tall on a gable-end.

Another whistles mañana,
Mañana, the station's lost and found
As he turns and twiddles the radio.
Initiate in the mysteries of contraflow,
He leads the cone-gatherers.

A third practises arcana,
Parting secrets from the sodden ground,
Strip-searching drystone walls
Where the yearning curlew calls
Cour-lee cour-lee.

From the vroom of a Fiesta,
Mañana, mañana, mañana,
A half-glimpse of roadmen
With their salad of chickweed and fat-hen;
On a tar brazier three sizzling snails,
Helix aspera.

A Landscape

Full-throated moon, porchlight
To the bone-strewn lair. Tosh?
Not so. I could use my torch as a cosh,
Having no need of torchlight,

Should I encounter thief or worse.
Moonlight stroking hair might shock
By stroking backwards, hair run amok.
The innkeeper had hinted at a curse.

Yet when I heard a howl in the wood,
No need to change direction:
I had garlic for protection
At throat and balls, so that was good.

Or maybe I'd misremembered?
Garlic for wolf, cross for bat.
Might I be off-beam on that?
Better a detour than dismembered.

Next thing I heard was a shout,
Definitely human, more like town crier
Than werewolf or vampire.
The moon had brought some revellers out.

Not so. The innkeeper had turned coat
And set upon my pungent trail
Garlic thieves. They never fail.
'Oyez!' they cry, and lunge at balls and throat.